DATE DUE

SEP 2 5 2013	
OCT 2 4 2015	
APR 11 2017	

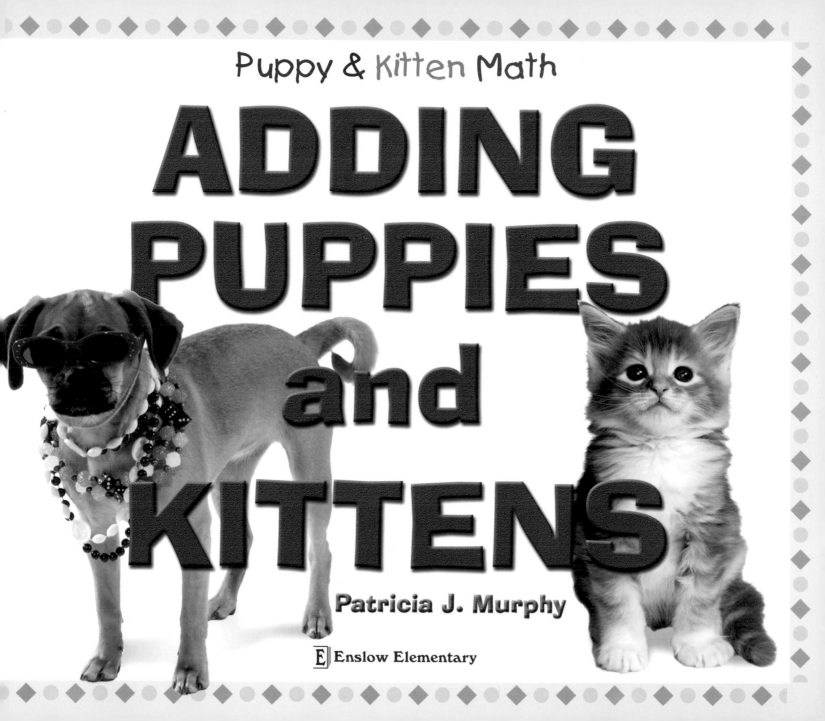

Puppy & Kitten Math

ADDING PUPPIES and KITTENS

Patricia J. Murphy

Enslow Elementary

Contents

Words to Know

addend—One number that is added to another number.

equal—To have the same number or value.

number—A word (such as *one* or *two*) or symbol (such as 1 or 2) used for counting, adding, subtracting, and more.

sum—The total from adding two or more numbers. It is also called the answer.

3

Adding Things

Adding is a way of putting together two or more **numbers**. The answer tells you how many things, like puppies or kittens, you have in all.

3

3 + 2 is an addition fact. You can write addition facts two ways:

addends

$$3$$
$$+\ 2$$
$$\overline{}$$
$$5$$

$$3 + 2 = 5$$

sum

+ 2 = 5

Every addition fact has four parts:

3 and **2** are **addends**. They are the numbers you add together.

+ means **plus**, or **add**.

= or ____ means **equals**.

5 is the **sum**, or answer.

Adding 0

3 + 0 play tag.

3   +   0

Use the
number line
to help you
add. Start at
3. Move right
0 spaces. The
sum is 3.

0   1   2   3   4   5   6   7   8   9

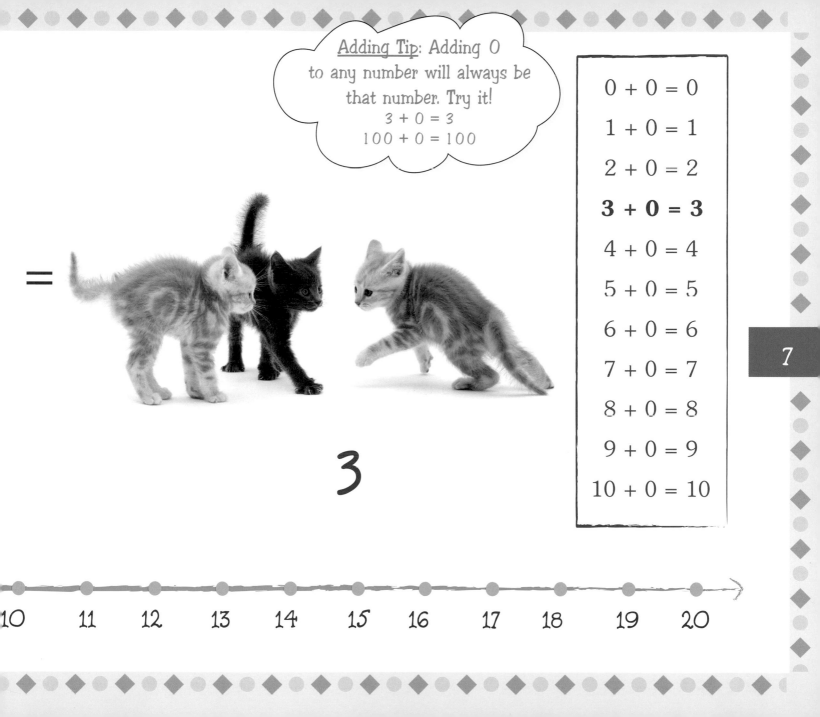

Adding Tip: Adding 0 to any number will always be that number. Try it!

$3 + 0 = 3$
$100 + 0 = 100$

$= 3$

$0 + 0 = 0$
$1 + 0 = 1$
$2 + 0 = 2$
$3 + 0 = 3$
$4 + 0 = 4$
$5 + 0 = 5$
$6 + 0 = 6$
$7 + 0 = 7$
$8 + 0 = 8$
$9 + 0 = 9$
$10 + 0 = 10$

7

10   11   12   13   14   15   16   17   18   19   20

Adding 1

2 + 1 tails wag.

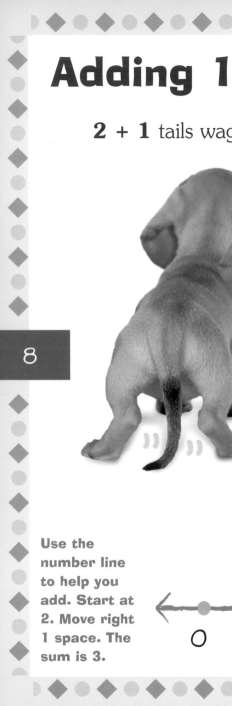

2   +   1

Use the number line to help you add. Start at 2. Move right 1 space. The sum is 3.

0   1   2   3   4   5   6   7   8   9

Adding Tip: Adding 1 to any number will always make the number one more. See for yourself!

5 + 1 = 6

6 is 1 more than 5.

=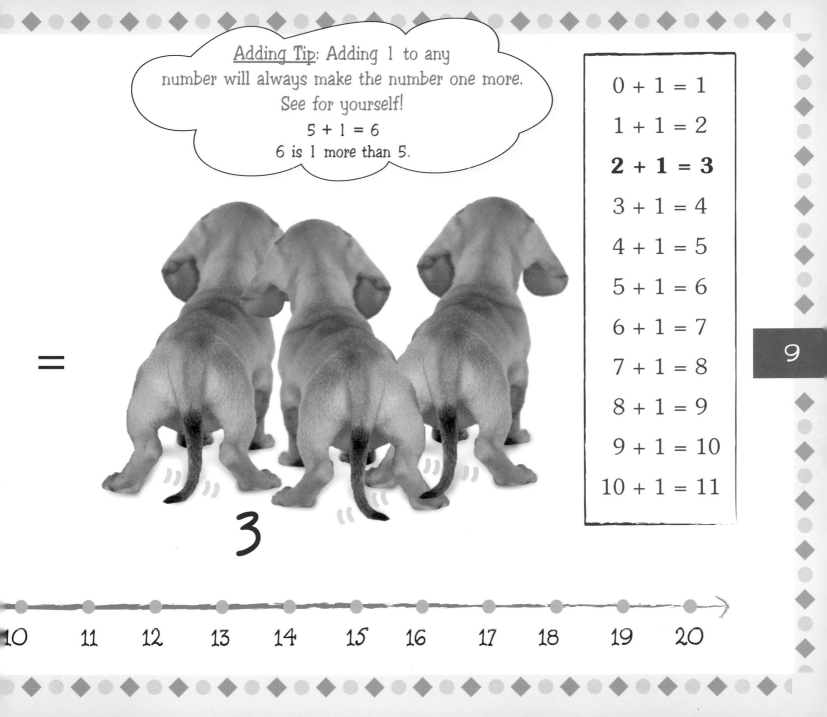

3

0 + 1 = 1

1 + 1 = 2

2 + 1 = 3

3 + 1 = 4

4 + 1 = 5

5 + 1 = 6

6 + 1 = 7

7 + 1 = 8

8 + 1 = 9

9 + 1 = 10

10 + 1 = 11

10   11   12   13   14   15   16   17   18   19   20

Adding 2

4 + 2 lick their paws.

4 + 2

Counting On

When you are adding more than 1, try counting on. It is one way to find the answers to addition facts. Try it with 4 + 2. Start with 4. Then "count on" 2 more.

4 . . . 5 . . .6   So, 4 + 2 = 6

Use the number line to help you add.

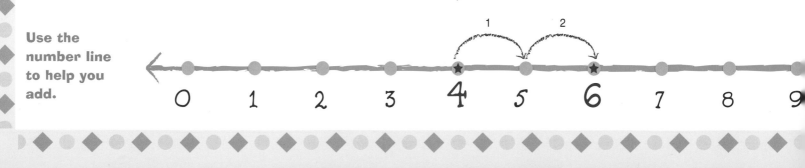

10

=

6

$0 + 2 = 2$

$1 + 2 = 3$

$2 + 2 = 4$

$3 + 2 = 5$

4 + 2 = 6

$5 + 2 = 7$

$6 + 2 = 8$

$7 + 2 = 9$

$8 + 2 = 10$

$9 + 2 = 11$

$10 + 2 = 12$

Adding Tip: You can "count on" with fingers, toes, objects, or a number line.

10   11   12   13   14   15   16   17   18   19   20

Adding 3

2 + 3 show their claws.

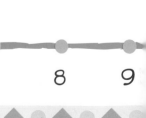

+

2

3

Use the number line to help you add.

0   1   2   3   4   5   6   7   8   9

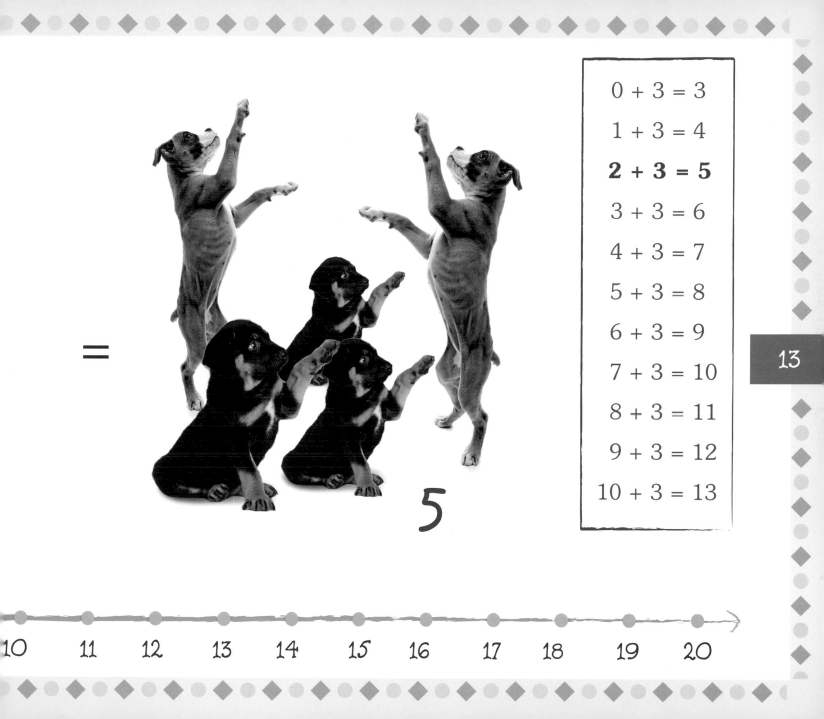

= 5

$$0 + 3 = 3$$
$$1 + 3 = 4$$
$$\mathbf{2 + 3 = 5}$$
$$3 + 3 = 6$$
$$4 + 3 = 7$$
$$5 + 3 = 8$$
$$6 + 3 = 9$$
$$7 + 3 = 10$$
$$8 + 3 = 11$$
$$9 + 3 = 12$$
$$10 + 3 = 13$$

10   11   12   13   14   15   16   17   18   19   20

Adding 4

5 + 4 play with toys.

5 + 4

Use the number line to help you add.

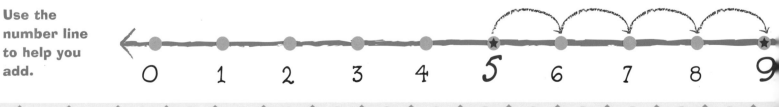

0 1 2 3 4 5 6 7 8 9

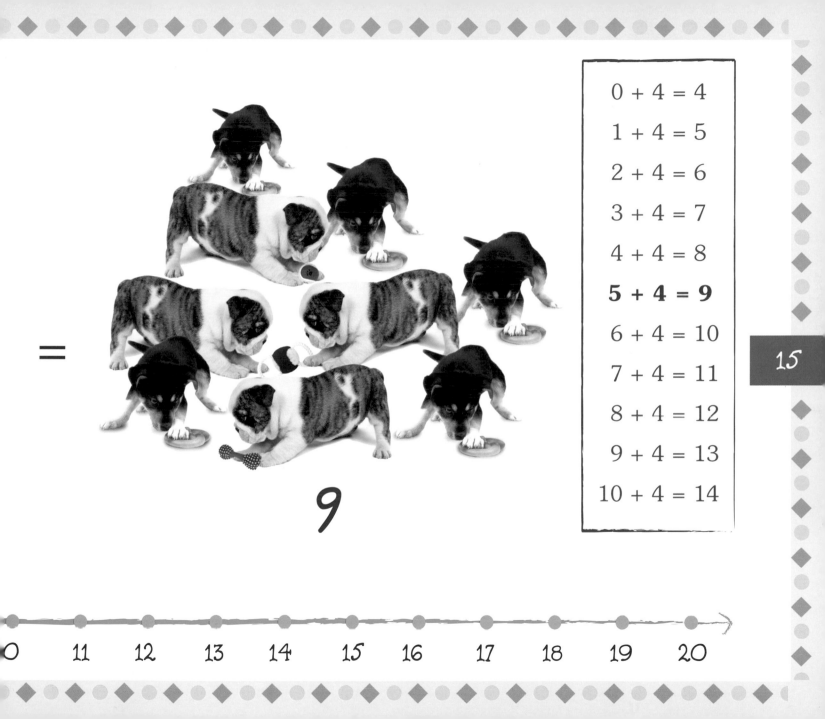

=

9

$$0 + 4 = 4$$
$$1 + 4 = 5$$
$$2 + 4 = 6$$
$$3 + 4 = 7$$
$$4 + 4 = 8$$
$$\mathbf{5 + 4 = 9}$$
$$6 + 4 = 10$$
$$7 + 4 = 11$$
$$8 + 4 = 12$$
$$9 + 4 = 13$$
$$10 + 4 = 14$$

15

0   11   12   13   14   15   16   17   18   19   20

Adding 5

2 + 5 climb in trees.

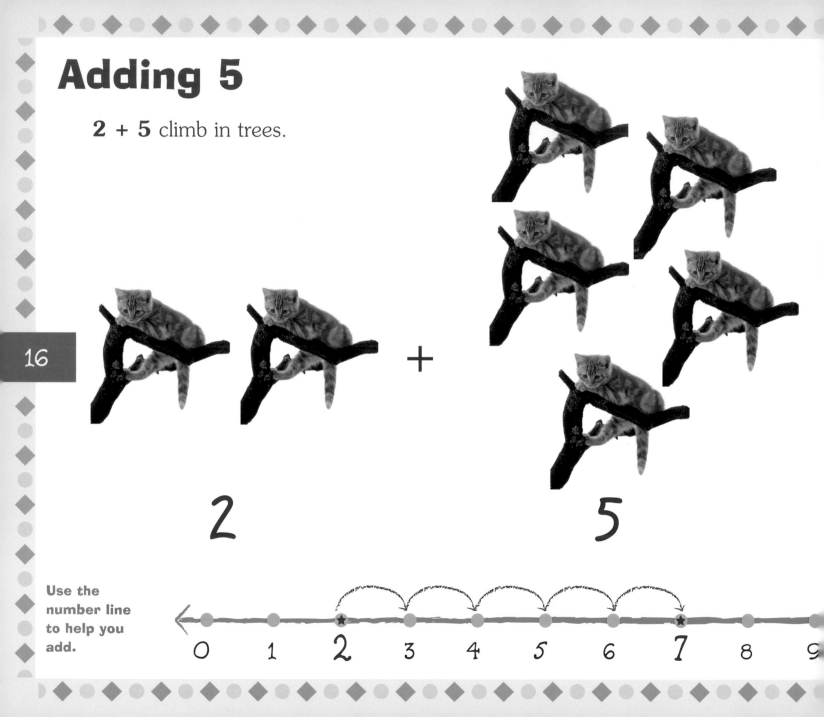

2

+

5

Use the number line to help you add.

0   1   2   3   4   5   6   7   8   9

5 + 5 is a doubles fact. Learn these doubles and you will know 10 new addition facts. ▌▌▌➡

1 + 1 = 2	6 + 6 = 12
2 + 2 = 4	7 + 7 = 14
3 + 3 = 6	8 + 8 = 16
4 + 4 = 8	9 + 9 = 18
5 + 5 = 10	10 + 10 = 20

0 + 5 = 5

1 + 5 = 6

2 + 5 = 7

3 + 5 = 8

4 + 5 = 9

5 + 5 = 10

6 + 5 = 11

7 + 5 = 12

8 + 5 = 13

9 + 5 = 14

10 + 5 = 15

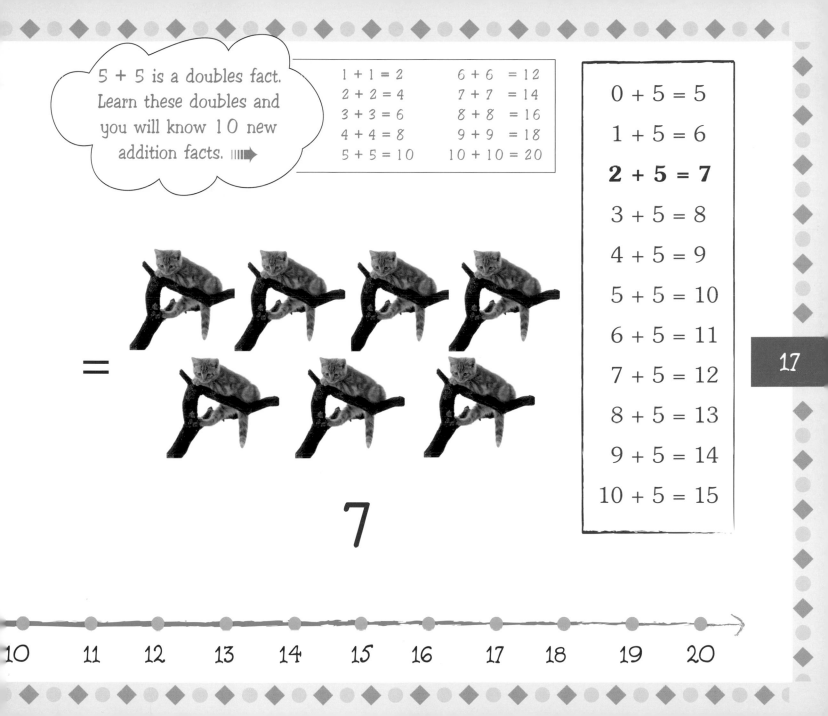

=

7

10   11   12   13   14   15   16   17   18   19   20

Adding 6

3 + 6 play piano keys.

3   6

Use the number line to help you add.

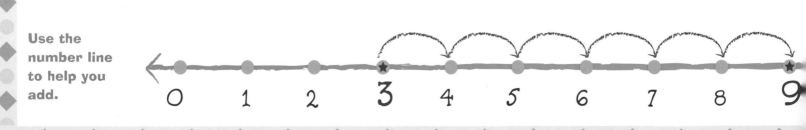

0   1   2   3   4   5   6   7   8   9

6 + 3 is the same as 3 + 6.
When you know one addition fact,
you really know two.

$$0 + 6 = 6$$
$$1 + 6 = 7$$
$$2 + 6 = 8$$
$$\mathbf{3 + 6 = 9}$$
$$4 + 6 = 10$$
$$5 + 6 = 11$$
$$6 + 6 = 12$$
$$7 + 6 = 13$$
$$8 + 6 = 14$$
$$9 + 6 = 15$$
$$10 + 6 = 16$$

=

9

0 11 12 13 14 15 16 17 18 19 20

Adding 7

1 + 7 wait for the vet.

+

1

7

Use the
number line
to help you
add.

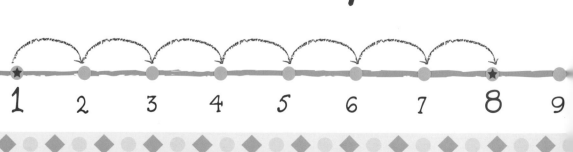

0   1   2   3   4   5   6   7   8   9

=

8

0 + 7 = 7

1 + 7 = 8

2 + 7 = 9

3 + 7 = 10

4 + 7 = 11

5 + 7 = 12

6 + 7 = 13

7 + 7 = 14

8 + 7 = 15

9 + 7 = 16

10 + 7 = 17

0   11   12   13   14   15   16   17   18   19   20

Adding 8

2 + 8 get all wet.

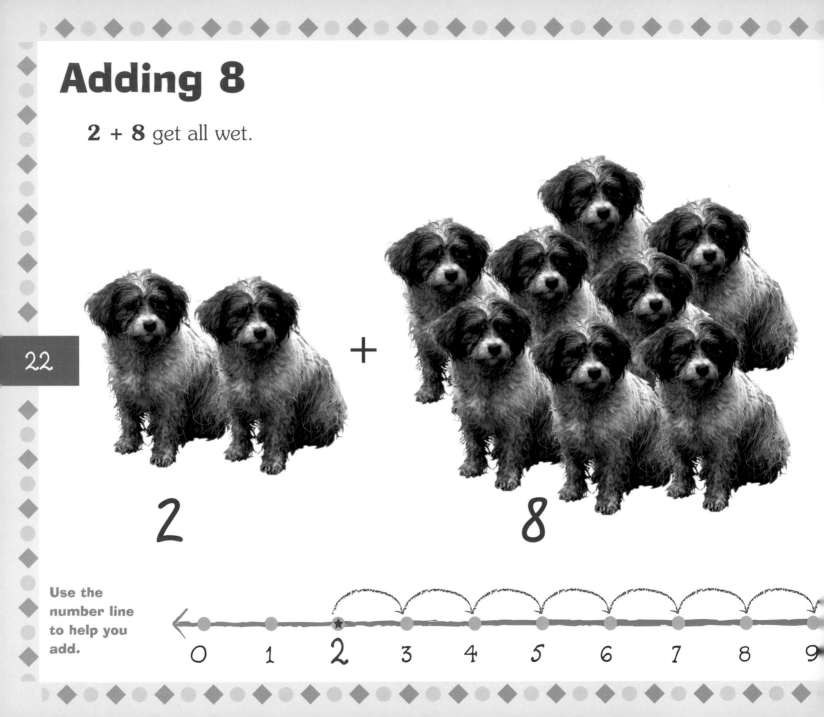

2

+

8

Use the
number line
to help you
add.

0   1   2   3   4   5   6   7   8   9

22

Learn all the facts that add up to 10. Soon you will know 11 new facts.

0 + 10 = 10	3 + 7 = 10
10 + 0 = 10	7 + 3 = 10
1 + 9 = 10	4 + 6 = 10
9 + 1 = 10	6 + 4 = 10
2 + 8 = 10	5 + 5 = 10
8 + 2 = 10	

=

10

0 + 8 = 8

1 + 8 = 9

2 + 8 = 10

3 + 8 = 11

4 + 8 = 12

5 + 8 = 13

6 + 8 = 14

7 + 8 = 15

8 + 8 = 16

9 + 8 = 17

10 + 8 = 18

23

10 11 12 13 14 15 16 17 18 19 20

Adding 9

1 + 9 try to hide.

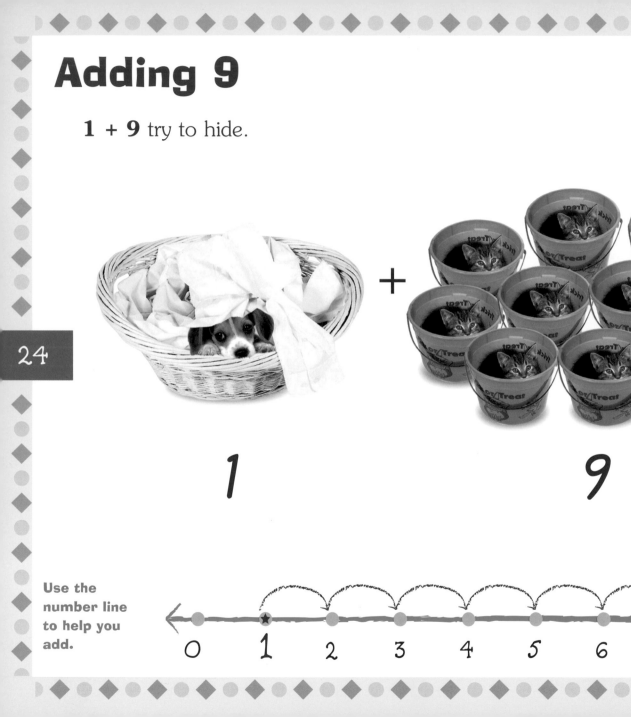

1

+

9

Use the
number line
to help you
add.

0   1   2   3   4   5   6   7   8   9

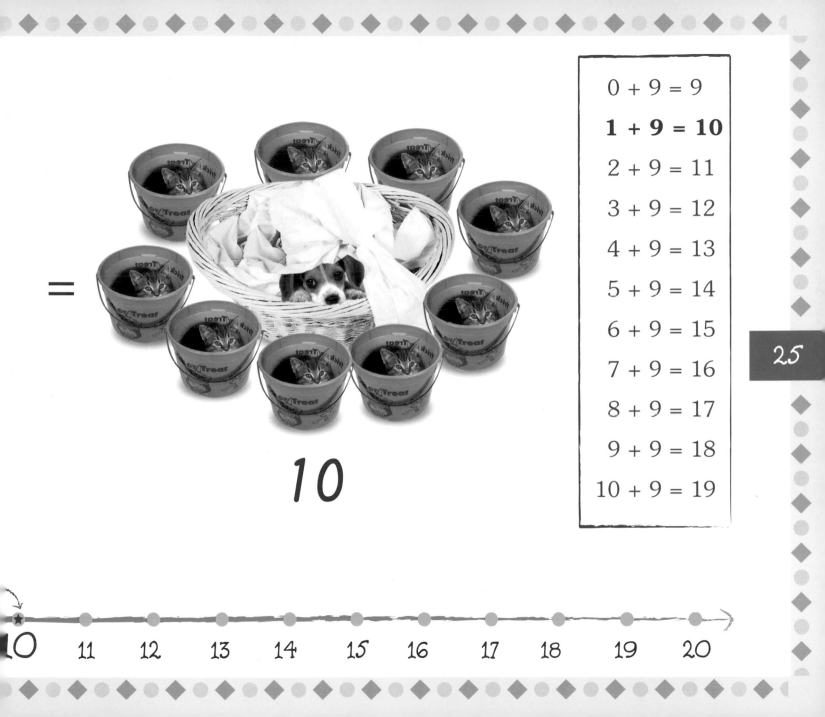

$=$

10

$0 + 9 = 9$

1 + 9 = 10

$2 + 9 = 11$

$3 + 9 = 12$

$4 + 9 = 13$

$5 + 9 = 14$

$6 + 9 = 15$

$7 + 9 = 16$

$8 + 9 = 17$

$9 + 9 = 18$

$10 + 9 = 19$

10 11 12 13 14 15 16 17 18 19 20

Adding 10

0 + 10 catch a ride. Bye! Bye!

+

0

10

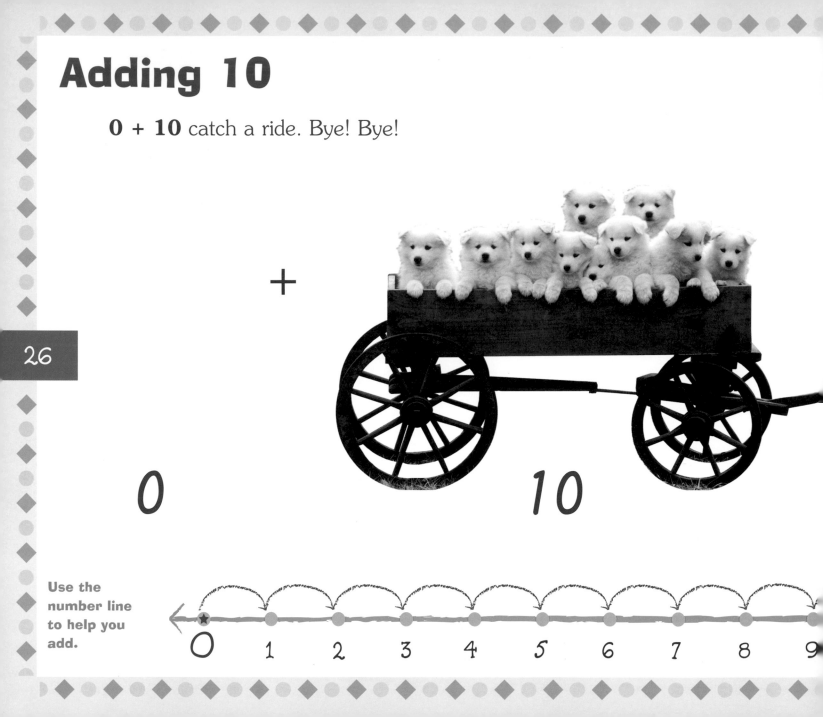

Use the number line to help you add.

0   1   2   3   4   5   6   7   8   9

=

10

0	**+ 10**	**=**	**10**
1	+ 10	=	11
2	+ 10	=	12
3	+ 10	=	13
4	+ 10	=	14
5	+ 10	=	15
6	+ 10	=	16
7	+ 10	=	17
8	+ 10	=	18
9	+ 10	=	19
10	+ 10	=	20

10 11 12 13 14 15 16 17 18 19 20

Looking Back

Take another look at the addition facts in this book.

+0
0 + 0 = 0	3 + 0 = 3	6 + 0 = 6	9 + 0 = 9
1 + 0 = 1	4 + 0 = 4	7 + 0 = 7	10 + 0 = 10
2 + 0 = 2	5 + 0 = 5	8 + 0 = 8	

+1
0 + 1 = 1	3 + 1 = 4	6 + 1 = 7	9 + 1 = 10
1 + 1 = 2	4 + 1 = 5	7 + 1 = 8	10 + 1 = 11
2 + 1 = 3	5 + 1 = 6	8 + 1 = 9	

28

+2
0 + 2 = 2	3 + 2 = 5	6 + 2 = 8	9 + 2 = 11
1 + 2 = 3	4 + 2 = 6	7 + 2 = 9	10 + 2 = 12
2 + 2 = 4	5 + 2 = 7	8 + 2 = 10	

+3
0 + 3 = 3	3 + 3 = 6	6 + 3 = 9	9 + 3 = 12
1 + 3 = 4	4 + 3 = 7	7 + 3 = 10	10 + 3 = 13
2 + 3 = 5	5 + 3 = 8	8 + 3 = 11	

+4
0 + 4 = 4	3 + 4 = 7	6 + 4 = 10	9 + 4 = 13
1 + 4 = 5	4 + 4 = 8	7 + 4 = 11	10 + 4 = 14
2 + 4 = 6	5 + 4 = 9	8 + 4 = 12	

+5
0 + 5 = 5	3 + 5 = 8	6 + 5 = 11	9 + 5 = 14
1 + 5 = 6	4 + 5 = 9	7 + 5 = 12	10 + 5 = 15
2 + 5 = 7	5 + 5 = 10	8 + 5 = 13	

+6

0 + 6 = 6	3 + 6 = 9	6 + 6 = 12	9 + 6 = 15
1 + 6 = 7	4 + 6 = 10	7 + 6 = 13	10 + 6 = 16
2 + 6 = 8	5 + 6 = 11	8 + 6 = 14	

+7

0 + 7 = 7	3 + 7 = 10	6 + 7 = 13	9 + 7 = 16
1 + 7 = 8	4 + 7 = 11	7 + 7 = 14	10 + 7 = 17
2 + 7 = 9	5 + 7 = 12	8 + 7 = 15	

+8

0 + 8 = 8	3 + 8 = 11	6 + 8 = 14	9 + 8 = 17
1 + 8 = 9	4 + 8 = 12	7 + 8 = 15	10 + 8 = 18
2 + 8 = 10	5 + 8 = 13	8 + 8 = 16	

+9

0 + 9 = 9	3 + 9 = 12	6 + 9 = 15	9 + 9 = 18
1 + 9 = 10	4 + 9 = 13	7 + 9 = 16	10 + 9 = 19
2 + 9 = 11	5 + 9 = 14	8 + 9 = 17	

+10

0 + 10 = 10	3 + 10 = 13	6 + 10 = 16	9 + 10 = 19
1 + 10 = 11	4 + 10 = 14	7 + 10 = 17	10 + 10 = 20
2 + 10 = 12	5 + 10 = 15	8 + 10 = 18	

Doubles

0 + 0 = 0	3 + 3 = 6	6 + 6 = 12	9 + 9 = 18
1 + 1 = 2	4 + 4 = 8	7 + 7 = 14	10 + 10 = 20
2 + 2 = 4	5 + 5 = 10	8 + 8 = 16	

Ways to Keep Adding

Write Your Own Adding Book

On each page, write a different addition fact. Draw a picture to go with each fact. Put the pages together. Share your addition book with friends.

Add Numbers Everywhere

Wherever you find numbers add them together. Add speed limits, numbers on license plates, and the numbers of your phone number all together. Think of other things you can add together—and then add them!

Roll and Add

Get a pair of dice, two pencils, and a piece of paper. Take turns rolling the dice with a friend. Write down the two numbers you roll and create addition facts with them. Take turns answering the addition facts.

Did Someone Say Turn Around?

Go through the book again with a friend. Take turns reading a math fact and saying its turn-around fact (4 + 2 = 6; 2 + 4 = 6). Have the person who says the turn-around fact turn around as he or she says it.

Rock, Paper, Add!

Instead of playing "rocks, paper, scissors," use your fingers to add numbers together. Ask a friend to play with you. First have each player make a fist. At the count of three, have each player show a number of fingers. Take turns adding the number of fingers together. Count the fingers to check your answers.

Learn More

Books

Bailer, Darice. *Josh Counts*. New York: Little Simon, 2002.

Brimner, Larry Dane. *Elwood's Bath*. Chanhassen, Minn.: Child's World, 2005.

———. *Max's Math Machine*. Chanhassen, Minn.: Child's World, 2005.

———. *Rumble Bus*. Chanhassen, Minn.: Child's World, 2005.

McGrath, Barbara Barbieri. *The M&M's Brand Addition Book*. Watertown, Mass.: Charlesbridge, 2004.

Murphy, Stuart J. *Get Up and Go!* New York: HarperCollins, 1996.

Nayer, Judy. *Adding It Up at the Zoo*. Mankato, MN: Yellow Umbrella Books, 2002.

Web Sites

All About Addition
www.aaamath.com/add.html

Fun Brain Numbers
www.funbrain.com/numbers.html

A Plus Math
www.aplusmath.com

Index

Series Math Consultant
Eileen Fernández, Ph.D.
Associate Professor, Mathematics Education
Montclair State University
Montclair, NJ

Series Literacy Consultant
Allan A. De Fina, Ph.D.
Past President of the New Jersey Reading Association
Professor, Department of Literacy Education
New Jersey City University
Jersey City, NJ

For people who ADD puppies and kittens to their lives

Acknowledgments: The author thanks Arlington Heights School District #25, in Arlington Heights, IL, and Lake Forest School District #67, in Lake Forest, IL, for their assistance in the research of this book.

Enslow Elementary, an imprint of Enslow Publishers, Inc.

Enslow Elementary® is a registered trademark of Enslow Publishers, Inc.

Library of Congress Cataloging-in-Publication Data

Murphy, Patricia J., 1963–
     Adding puppies and kittens / by Patricia J. Murphy.
          p. cm. — (Puppy and kitten math)
     Includes bibliographical references and index.
     ISBN-13: 978-0-7660-2726-8
     ISBN-10: 0-7660-2726-0
     1. Addition—Juvenile literature. 2. Arithmetic—Juvenile literature. I. Title.
     QA115.M858 2007
     513.2'11—dc22   2006004833

Printed in the United States of America

10 9 8 7 6 5 4 3 2

To Our Readers: We have done our best to make sure all Internet Addresses in this book were active and appropriate when we went to press. However, the author and the publisher have no control over and assume no liability for the material available on those Internet sites or on other Web sites they may link to. Any comments or suggestions can be sent by e-mail to comments@enslow.com or to the address on the back cover.

Photo credits: Carolyn A. McKeone/Photo Researchers, Inc., pp. 8, 9; Hemera Technologies, pp. 1, 10–11, 20 puppies to left, kittens sitting, 14 #5, 15 puppy with disc, 20–21 vet, top left, bottom center, 24–25; © iStockphoto.com, pp. 20–21 second kitten on bench (Alon Brik); 20–21 bench (Anthony P. Cortizas, Jr.); 3 puppy to right (Gary Caviness); 20–21 puppy with cast (Jan Quist); 4 #4, 5 bulldog puppy (Justin Horrocks); 3 kitten standing (Mark Hayes); 20–21 puppy with bucket (Ryan KC Wong); 20–21 top right (Stephanie Phillips); 20–21 bottom right (Thomas Steinke); © Natzbaer/Dreamstime.com, p. 5 puppies; © 2000 Photo Disc, Inc., pp. 4, 5 kittens; Shutterstock, pp. 12, 13; Steve Lied/Dreamstime.com, pp. 22–23; © SuperStock, Inc./Superstock, pp. 18, 19, 26–27; © Warren Photographics, pp. 6, 7, 16, 17.

Cover photo: © Warren Photographics

Enslow Elementary
an imprint of
Enslow Publishers, Inc.
40 Industrial Road
Box 398
Berkeley Heights, NJ 07922
USA
http://www.enslow.com